Original title:

Life's Purpose: Somewhere Between Snacks and Naps

Copyright © 2025 Creative Arts Management OÜ
All rights reserved.

Author: Evelyn Hartman
ISBN HARDBACK: 978-1-80566-251-8
ISBN PAPERBACK: 978-1-80566-546-5

Pondering the Peach

In the orchard where I dream,
I ponder fruits, or so it seems.
Do they taste the sun's sweet glow?
Or just hang out, taking flow?

With every bite, a thought takes flight,
Should I binge on fruit or nap tonight?
A juicy peach, oh what a tease,
Perhaps I'll loaf and take it easy, please!

Now the juice drips down my chin,
Is indulging peachy bliss a sin?
I laugh aloud, my tummy's full,
Simple joys are never dull!

So as I ponder each bite and sip,
The secret's out, I've found my trip.
In fruit and sleep, I find my way,
Oh, what a fabulous, funny day!

A Soothing Slice of Time

A slice of cake, a comfy chair,
I'm lost in sugar, void of care.
The world can spin, the clock can tick,
But I'm just here, indulging a trick.

With frosting swirls, my worries fade,
Each nibble's laughter, my own parade.
Forget the chores, they're on hold,
I'm living sweetly, bold and gold.

When nap time calls, I heed the grace,
A snug embrace in my happy place.
Time slips away like frosting's drip,
I float on dreams, let my troubles skip.

So here's a toast to cake and snooze,
For in the silly, there's much to choose.
A playful heart, a giggle or two,
In delightful daze, we'll make it through!

Laughter Over Leftovers

In the fridge, a feast awaits,
Old pizza looks like it's in states.
But laughter bubbles, warms the soul,
As I munch on joy, that's my goal.

Soup from last week, a daring quest,
Should I eat it? Well, I jest!
With each slurp, a story unfolds,
In the depths of laughter, life beholds.

The Sublime Simplicity of Rest

Nap time calls, a cozy zone,
Snuggled deep in my fluffy throne.
The world outside spins fast and wild,
Here I'm a calm, contented child.

Dreams of snacks float in the air,
Chips and dips without a care.
In every snooze, a giggle found,
As snacks and dreams dance all around.

The Half-Eaten Journey

A sandwich gone, just crust remains,
I ponder life, through cheese-stained lanes.
Each bite reveals a path anew,
Where snacks and naps film a view.

Potato chips scattered like stars,
Leading to memories, oh how bizarre!
Yet in each crunch, I find a light,
That fills my heart with sheer delight.

Moonlight and Munchies

Under the moon, a snack parade,
With cookies dancing, none dismayed.
Chasing crumbs in a wild delight,
Who needs sleep on this starry night?

With laughter echoing through the dark,
I munch on dreams, igniting a spark.
Each bite a giggle, a memory made,
Life's simple joys, serenely played.

The Philosophy of a Cozy Chair

In a world of hustle, I find my zone,
That comfy chair is my favorite throne.
With snacks in hand and a fluffy throw,
I ponder deep thoughts about my next show.

The cushions wrap me like a warm embrace,
As I contemplate the meaning of my space.
Is it nap or snack? I can't decide,
But in this chair, I take it in stride.

Nourishment of the Soul

Chips and dips are my kind of feast,
They fill me up and never leave me least.
A crunch of joy, a sip of cheer,
In simple pleasures, I persevere.

Chocolate whispers sweet nothings to me,
Like a friend who knows exactly what to be.
Each bite a hug from the universe wide,
Reminding me that happiness is bona fide.

Bites of Balance

I juggle snacks like a circus act,
With nachos here, and cookies stacked.
Balancing crumbs on my nose so fine,
Takes skill, precision, and a bit of wine.

I search for order in this playful mess,
With pretzels and popcorn, I feel so blessed.
Life is a buffet, my friends, don't you see?
In every morsel, there's pure glee.

The Calming Crave

When the world gets loud, I close my eyes,
Visualizing pizza with extra fries.
Each craving whispers, 'Come and indulge,'
While nap time beckons, my eyelids bulge.

Be it salty or sweet, my tastes roam free,
As I drift off to snack-induced reverie.
In dreams, I frolic through fields of delight,
In a culinary wonderland, far from sight.

Finding Zen in the Snacks

In a world of chip crunches,
I seek the peace in pops and pans.
With every munch of crispy bites,
I find my calm in snacky plans.

Oh, the nacho cheese's embrace,
Brings serenity to my evening snack.
To find my zen in guacamole,
Is truly the best way to relax.

Ice cream dreams in sunny bowls,
Sprinkles shower down like love.
Each scoop a taste of pure delight,
It's heaven sent from above.

So here I sit, with crumbs and cheers,
A meditation on my plate.
With every sip of fizzy drinks,
I discover joy, I contemplate.

Forkfuls of Wonder

I raise my fork to greet the day,
With pasta twists and garlic bread.
Each bite a sprinkle of delight,
In my culinary quest, I'm led.

The sauce is sticky, flavors dance,
A ravioli of pure romance.
With pesto dreams and cheese galore,
I savor, twirl, and take a chance.

Dessert arrives, a pie so grand,
An apple slice, a berry cream.
I fork through wonders, thick and sweet,
In every bite, I find my dream.

So fork it up and spread the joy,
With whipped cream clouds and cake galore.
In every meal, I find the fun,
A tasty life, forevermore.

The Pause Between Moments

In the kitchen, chaos reigns,
Water boils and timers beep.
I take a breath, then add a spice,
Then feel the chatter, laugh, and leap.

For in the pause, I take a snack,
A crumble here, a morsel there.
Between the chopping and the stir,
I find my joy in gooey fare.

A moment's break to taste and think,
Chocolate chips in cookie dough.
With each sweet bite, I realize,
The little joys make life a show.

So pause a while, enjoy the treat,
And let the flavors fill your soul.
In every nibble, laugh, and cheer,
You'll find the moments make you whole.

Culinary Clouded Thoughts

With a whisk in hand, I ponder deep,
The mysteries of butter and bread.
Cloudy thoughts mix with flour dust,
As visions of pastries dance in my head.

Oh, where does time go in the kitchen?
As muffins rise and cookies melt.
In this whirlwind of sweet delights,
I lose my thoughts, a jumbled belt.

A sprinkle here, a dash of joy,
The mix of chaos fuels my heart.
With every bake, I giggle loud,
In this funny dance, I play my part.

So embrace the scatter, the tasty thrill,
And let the humor guide your hand.
In every bite, a laugh unfolds,
Culinary bliss, life is so grand.

Hibernating Between Bites

In the cozy nook of my favorite chair,
Chips and salsa waiting, beyond compare.
A stretch, a yawn, I settle in tight,
Nibbling and snoozing, all feels so right.

The couch is my kingdom, snacks by the throne,
Where every crumb feels like a rare gemstone.
A snooze here and there, then back for a bite,
This dance of delight is my idea of flight.

Laughter erupts from a sitcom's embrace,
Between bites and half-dreams, I find my place.
Air-popped corn flies, I hoot like a fool,
Mastering snacks while I play the cool.

As evening descends and I've had my fill,
I curl like a cat, every nap worth the thrill.
My heart gives a wink as I drift into dreams,
Of mountains of snacks and rivers of creams.

The Zen of Nibbles and Naps

Seated in serenity, snacks piled high,
M&Ms and gummy bears catching my eye.
A crunch and a munch, then a soft, tender sigh,
The path to enlightenment, I'd truly imply.

With every morsel, my mind starts to clear,
Harmony found in the crunch so sincere.
Dreams mixed with flavors, a joyful requiem,
A cookie's sweet whisper, a nut's gentle hymn.

The world fades away, it's just me and treats,
Where the only agenda's to savor what's sweet.
With cookies for wisdom and soft drinks for cheer,
I laugh as I loiter, no worries near.

In this moment of bliss, I stick with my goals,
Naps and good snacks make the best of our roles.
So I ponder and munch, my wise heart aglow,
Finding truth in the flavors that twirl to and fro.

Whispers of the Afternoon Slumber

A gentle hum beckons my eyelids to close,
With a plush blanket wrapped, in my snack-filled prose.
Popcorn golden dreams take over the scene,
As I drift between moments, both silly and serene.

The clock ticks along, time's a friend and a foe,
Between munching and napping, the seconds move slow.
Traces of laughter dance through the air,
With each crispy bite, I float without care.

The lounge chair embraces me, comfy and wide,
While chips play the DJ, my sweet, crispy guide.
In this whimsical zone, all worries take flight,
As dreams blend with munchies, in pure, silly delight.

So here's to the moments of joy and of fluff,
Where nibbles and nap times remind me I'm tough.
With a wink to the snack gods and a sway to the breeze,
I roll into slumber, with giggles and ease.

Morsels of Meaning

In the fridge, what do I see?
A snack that's laughing at me!
Popcorn dancing with delight,
I'll munch and crunch into the night.

Is it chips, or is it cake?
Decisions make my tummy ache.
With every bite, I ponder deep,
Is life just snacks and naps, or sleep?

Gummy bears sing in the bowl,
Chocolate whispers, 'I am whole.'
Each flavor tells a silly tale,
In this buffet, I will prevail.

Between each snack, a tiny snooze,
Dreaming of my next-cheesy muse.
For in this feast of tasty fun,
I find my heart, my soul, my sun.

Soft Pillows of Reflection

Nestled in a cozy chair,
Dreams drift gently through the air.
The world outside can wait and see,
As I nap munching on a brie.

Moments stretch like warm macaroni,
With each nibble, I feel less phony.
Visions dance like pudding sweet,
On this sofa, I find my beat.

Cuddles call like cookie dough,
I snooze and snack, my heart aglow.
Each soft pillow a hug divine,
In comfort's arms, I intertwine.

Bite of laughter, spoon of sigh,
In these moments, I touch the sky.
Let time slip by, let worries wane,
As snacks and naps flow like a train.

A Pause in the Feast

Halt! A snack, it pulls my hand,
Cheesy puffs, oh, what a band!
The feast can wait, that I decree,
For every crunch brings glee to me.

One more bite, then I'll reflect,
Is it snacks, or is it elect?
With nachos stacked, I sway and dip,
This cheesy moment is my script.

Take a break, a sip of juice,
Life's little joys, I shall deduce.
In this parade of tasty treats,
I find my rhythm, my fun beats.

Each pause a treasure, each gulp a tale,
In laughter's echo, I shall prevail.
Embracing munchies with a nap,
I find my joy in every flap.

Tidbits of Tranquility

Whispers of cookies call my name,
In this soothing snack-time game.
Crunchy snacks and slumbers tight,
Savoring fun, in morning light.

A sprinkle here, a dollop there,
Mixing flavors, life's affair.
With every nibble, I embrace,
A calmness settles in this space.

Donuts bring a sweet refrain,
While soft pillows cheer in vain.
Maybe it's all just a big charade,
But in this treat, I've got it made.

As the clock ticks out the day,
I savor bites and drift away.
For tidbits small bring peace untold,
In every snack, a joy unfolds.

Crumbs of Contentment

In the crannies of the couch, they lie,
A treasure trove of chips and pie.
Morsels left by evening's feast,
A crispy gift from my snacky beast.

I munch on dreams that softly hum,
As nap time calls, I start to succumb.
With crumbs of joy upon my lap,
I sink into a cozy nap.

The fridge whispers secrets of delight,
While visions of donuts dance at night.
Euphoria in every bite,
As my sleepy eyes close tight.

Sometimes a snack is all I need,
To nourish my soul and plant a seed.
In fluff and crumbs, I find my way,
In this delicious, goofy play.

The Art of Idling

Cushions creak as I recline,
Days drift by, all feels divine.
Remote in hand, my throne of rest,
I ponder which show is the best.

The clock keeps ticking, but I'm unfazed,
In this glorious haze, I'm amazed.
A blanket fort of cozy bliss,
Life's tasks denied, I simply dismiss.

With snacks galore, I make my stand,
A crispy chip in one hand.
Naps are art, relaxation's crown,
As I lounge like a lazy clown.

Recline, recline, no rush today,
Idleness? Oh, I'll gladly stay.
In sweet surrender, time shall pass,
While I indulge in my comfort grass.

Dreams in a Chip Bag

We gather round for chips and fun,
A party formed, the munchies won.
Each crunch we make, a laughter shared,
In our own world, we are prepared.

Flavors come alive with every bite,
In salty storms that feel so right.
The air is thick with eager snackers,
As thoughts float high, no room for slackers.

A chip, a dip, a giggle bloop,
I dream of feasts in this chippy group.
Naps may beckon, they can wait,
'Til every last crunch is on my plate.

In this bag, my dreams do soar,
With every nibble, I want more.
So pass the snacks and let's not stop,
This crunchy joy, I'll take the top!

Embracing the Sweet Surrender

Sugar rushes through the air,
Gummies dancing without a care.
Today I choose what makes me glee,
In a candy-coated reverie.

The world is vast, with tasks galore,
But here I 'rest' on the candy floor.
Each piece a promise, a fleeting giggle,
As I munch and snack, then twist and wiggle.

Naps creep in like chocolate fudge,
Whispering softly, "There's no need to judge."
Surrender sweetened, I melt with ease,
In this candy haze, I'm sure to please.

So lift your snacks and toast the day,
In laughter and treats, let us sway.
For happiness lies in sugary spins,
In snacks and naps where joy begins.

The Comfortable Drift

Amidst the couch, a gentle sway,
With chips and dip, I spend my day.
A nap slips in, a snack slips out,
In this fine dance, no trace of doubt.

The remote's my friend, the pillow's tight,
I wander dreams in cozy light.
Each munch a melody, each yawn a sigh,
In this simple bliss, I happily lie.

Time ticks slowly, like melted cheese,
With silly shows, I aim to please.
In every crunch, a little laugh,
Finding joy in a lazy path.

So here I sit, with snacks on hand,
In dreamland realms, so unplanned.
The world outside can wait its turn,
For couch and snacks, my heart will yearn.

Lullabies and Licorice

Sweet lullabies in candy dreams,
Licorice whispers, or so it seems.
A sugary quest while I recline,
To taste the stars, and drink the wine.

My bed transformed to a candy throne,
With wrappers crinkled, I am alone.
Snoozing softly, snacks abound,
In sugary realms, my joy is found.

Chocolate rivers and popcorn skies,
I drift through flavors, oh how time flies.
Counting each candy, one by one,
In this sweet life, I find my fun.

So let me nap as flavors merge,
In this sweet world where dreams emerge.
Between the laughs and candy streams,
I find my purpose in silly dreams.

Cravings of the Comfortable Heart

In the warmth of dusk, snacks abound,
On this plush throne, I am crowned.
Each munch a giggle, every crunch a cheer,
For tiny morsels bring joy near.

Flavored popcorn leaps in joy,
A silly dance, like a child's toy.
With every nibble, laughter grows,
In cravings deep, my spirit flows.

A choco-bar smile, a chip parade,
In this lazy haven, I'm unafraid.
The world flips mute, as I explore,
In my snack kingdom, who could ask for more?

So roll the credits, let's have a feast,
Where laughter's rich and worries cease.
In comfortable dreams of fun and art,
I thrive tomorrow with a happy heart.

A Feast for the Soul

Gather 'round, for food is near,
A feast of joy, oh bring the cheer!
With pizza slices, and soda bursts,
In happy bites, my soul it thirsts.

Laughing loudly, the chaos flows,
With every dish, my fondness grows.
Tacos tumble, fries may fly,
In this grand spread, we all comply.

Delightful treats on every plate,
The couch invites, let's celebrate.
A smorgasbord, for the merry heart,
In this fun meal, we all play a part.

So raise a chip to laugh and play,
In every crunch, we seize the day.
For snacks and joy, in playful swirl,
Bring purpose sweet to every world.

The Intermission of Dreams

In the realm of cozy chairs,
We contemplate our whims.
A snack to stave off grumbling,
A nap to soothe our limbs.

Thoughts of quests and worldly fame,
Are tenderly tossed aside.
For here we find a joy anew,
In slumber's gentle tide.

So linger in this lazy bliss,
Where time can stretch and yawn.
We'll dream of silly, sweet delights,
Until the light of dawn.

With crumbs upon our pillows,
And pillows soft and warm,
We sing a song of fluffy clouds,
And naps that take us far.

Whispers of Afternoon Delights

The afternoon sun beams gold,
As snacks dance on the plate.
We giggle at our lazy dreams,
With crumbs we celebrate.

A cup of tea, a muffin too,
In cozy nooks we hide.
The world can keep its busy plans,
We savor and abide.

With every bite a tiny cheer,
For each delightful sip.
A life of leisure calls our names,
As time begins to slip.

So let the clock tick gently on,
As whispers fill the air.
In this haven of pure joy,
Naps and snacks await our care.

In Search of Sweet Surrender

We wander through the pantry aisles,
In search of treats galore.
Chocolate, chips, and gummy bears,
Oh what a grand explore!

With wrappers crinkled 'neath our feet,
And crumbs upon our shirt,
We find our bliss in every bite,
A treasure with no hurt.

As eyelids grow heavy and warm,
We seek our soft retreat.
In shadows cast from midday sun,
We curl up, oh so sweet.

From snacks to naps, our journey sways,
In comfort's tender call.
We laugh, we munch, we dream away,
In this delightful sprawl.

The Art of Leisurely Moments

In the art of doing nothing,
We master each small break.
With snacks piled high in every hand,
We giggle as we shake.

A quick retreat to fluffy dreams,
To recharge our worn-out souls.
The couch becomes our kingdom vast,
With pillows as our tolls.

Each stretch and yawn a masterpiece,
As laughter fills the air.
We toast with sips of fizzy joy,
In our lazy, happy lair.

So find your spot and settle in,
Let the world spin and sway.
For snacks and naps are all we need,
To brighten up our day!

A Symphony of Snacks

In the pantry, I hear a tune,
Chips and cookies make me swoon.
Popcorn dances with a crunch,
As I prepare for my snack lunch.

The fridge hums a symphony,
Of yogurt, cheese, and mystery.
Bananas sing, all ripe and sweet,
In this concert, I find my seat.

With each bite, a note released,
My hunger fades, my joy increased.
A melody composed of taste,
In this harmony, no time to waste.

So let's feast like stars on stage,
In this act, we disengage.
No encore's needed, just one more,
As the snacks beckon, we adore.

Snack Time Revelations

In a world of chips and dip,
I ponder deeply on each sip.
Are nachos signs of hidden truths?
Or just a crunch that entertains our youth?

Candy bars, I muse with glee,
Are sweets the answer? Yes, indeed!
The gummy bears wave as they cheer,
Their sugary wisdom, perfectly clear.

A donut's glaze can spark a thought,
What have I learned from munching a lot?
Perhaps it's joy that fills the air,
With every bite, life's sweet affair.

So let us chew on wisdom's treat,
While cozying up to something sweet.
In snack time's revelry, we find,
The secrets that our hearts unwind.

The Sweetness of Stillness

In a quiet corner, snacks align,
I pause and savor every line.
A cookie crumbles, softly speaks,
It whispers secrets of cozy weeks.

A napkin catches crumbs of grace,
As I drift to a peaceful space.
Choco dreams swirl upon my lid,
In stillness, I find the joy I hid.

The cake awaits my gentle hand,
In this still life, I take a stand.
A sip of tea, a quiet cheer,
In munching moments, I find what's dear.

Each snack a treasure, taking its time,
In this calm, I find my rhyme.
With every nibble, the world does fade,
In stillness, the sweetest memories are made.

Chow Time Contemplations

What makes a meal divine, I ponder,
Is it flavors, or is it wonder?
A plate of fries might hold the key,
To answers that elude me.

As I munch on this tasty fare,
A burger's smile, beyond compare.
Do donuts dream of holes aglow?
Chow time brings thoughts that ebb and flow.

With every bites, a thought shall twirl,
Do pickles care in their green swirl?
As ketchup runs, a saucy friend,
What do we seek, or is it the blend?

So let's chew on life, both big and small,
In every bite, we heed the call.
Chow time's musings, perhaps renowned,
In snacks and nibbles, wisdom's found.

Whimsical Whiskers of Thought

In a world of fluff and flight,
Cats ponder snacks, both day and night.
With whimsical whiskers, they chase their dreams,
While plotting mischief with tiny schemes.

A nibble here, a nibble there,
They scheme and plot without a care.
Between the purrs and playful spry,
They nap and snack, oh my, oh my!

The sunbeam warms their royal throne,
As they prance and saunter, proud and prone.
With every snack, a nap is near,
In their fuzzy world, they feel no fear.

So let us giggle and sip our tea,
On this absurdity, we all agree.
For in the chaos, there lies delight,
Amidst the naps and those tasty bites.

Chewing on Dreams

Beneath the moon, the stars will gleam,
I sit and ponder over ice cream.
What is the secret, what does it mean?
To chew on dreams, both sweet and keen.

With a cookie crumbling in my hand,
I make bold plans; it's truly grand.
But hold on tight, as I take a bite,
These tender dreams may just take flight.

A nap awaits, should I dare to pause,
Lost in thought, like a slight hiccough's cause.
In slumber land, my ideas soar,
Then I wake startled, craving more.

So here I sit with crumbs and schemes,
Munching away at my daydreams.
In this quirky dance of snack and snooze,
I juggle my joys, my laughs, my muse.

Pockets of Peace

In pockets of peace, I find my place,
With a cookie tin, a joyful embrace.
Snug on the couch, a cozy retreat,
I nibble away, this simple feat.

The laughter echoes, my phone on mute,
As I pile the treats, oh what a hoot!
A sprinkle of chaos, a dash of fun,
With snacks for a year, I feel like I've won.

Naps call my name as I count my bites,
Floating on dreams through the starry nights.
In every morsel, a giggle divine,
Life's lighter moments, perfectly fine.

So gather the crumbs, and let's share a laugh,
In culinary dreams, we find our path.
For in this chaos, we all will find,
A slice of joy, both happy and kind.

Siesta and Sweets

A siesta, oh dreamy delight,
Plunge into pillows without a fight.
With sweets by my side, the world fades away,
As I drift on sugar clouds for the day.

Chocolate whispers in slumber's grasp,
Each dreamy bite is a gentle clasp.
With marshmallow dreams floating so high,
I giggle awake, to a sugar supply.

Between each snooze, a sprinkle of fun,
While cookies and giggles create quite the run.
So pass the gummies, the fudge, and the cream,
In this cheerful dance, let's munch and dream.

In siestas sweet, we find our play,
The snacks are calling, let's seize the day!
For laughter awaits in every treat,
In our cozy kingdom, life's truly sweet.

Dreamscapes Flavored with Cocoa

In the land where chocolate flows,
All my worries fade like snow.
Marshmallow clouds, fluffy and tight,
I dream of treats both day and night.

Bite-sized dreams in a cookie jar,
Running wild, a candy star.
With every sip of cocoa bliss,
I nibble fate and steal a kiss.

Frothy rivers, sweetened streams,
Wrapped in joy, I'm lost in dreams.
Giggles echo, laughter peaks,
In this zone, my heart just squeaks.

Waking up with crumbs on my face,
I contemplate my snack-filled space.
Coffee brews with a cheerful sigh,
Tomorrow's treats, oh my, oh my!

The Gentle Tug of Tasty Moments

A burden lifted with every bite,
Snack time brings a sheer delight.
Crackers crunching, laughter flows,
As chocolate drizzles, the happiness grows.

Gummy bears pull at my sleeve,
"Join us now!" they cheerfully weave.
Popcorn whispers, "Just a taste,"
In this sweet world, we're never faced.

Donuts circle like playful friends,
Round and round, the good times blend.
Pizza slices dance and sway,
In this feast, we live to play.

So let's relish all the fun,
In this quirky, snack-filled run.
Moments tug at my heartstrings,
In the joy that munching brings.

Mellow Moments on a Soft Bed

Feathered pillows, soft and sweet,
Alongside treats, the perfect seat.
In a haze of dreams and snacks,
I float on clouds, I've got no lacks.

Chocolate chip cookies hug me tight,
As naps whisper, "Stay till the night."
Fluffy dreams on a marshmallow sponge,
Resting here, I feel the plunge.

A cupcake chorus, gently hums,
Telling tales of all its crumbs.
Laughter springs from sugar highs,
While I chase after sweet sunrise.

So here I linger, soft and calm,
Beneath a sprinkle-showered palm.
Mellow vibes in blissful streams,
Wrapped in heaven, lost in dreams.

Cuddles and Crunches

In cozy corners, we gather 'round,
With crispy snacks, joy's profound.
Warm blankets wrapped, snug and tight,
Crunchy bites bring pure delight.

Chips and giggles fill the air,
Cuddled close, without a care.
Each crunch a giggle, every munch,
Creates a smile with every crunch.

Cheeseballs roll, a silly game,
Laughter spreads, joy is the aim.
Popcorn flies as cheers erupt,
In these cuddles, we're all enrapt.

So let the snacks and laughter flow,
In cozy hubs where friendships grow.
With every cuddle, every crunch,
We celebrate life, in every munch!

Unraveled Threads

In the chaos of the day, I roam,
Snack in one hand, I feel at home.
Between bites, a nap pulls tight,
I wrestle with dreams, both sweet and light.

Oh, the couch calls with its warm embrace,
I'll just close my eyes, it's a race!
A chirp from the fridge, a pizza pie,
This dance of hunger, oh my oh my!

Threads of ambition start to unwind,
As I ponder if chips are well-designed.
A snack for my thoughts, a nap for my soul,
In this wild journey, I take control.

But let's not forget, the joy they bring,
Every crunch a symphony, each snooze a fling.
So here we go, in this blissful trap,
Snacks and dreams, the ultimate map.

The Quiet Crunch of Reality

Mornings with cereal, a quiet delight,
Milk spills like problems, out of sight.
I chew on the woes of the day ahead,
But first, let me snack, then dream in my bed.

With chips as my armor, I conquer the grind,
And every little crunch, is a moment well-timed.
Naps are like clouds, they float away,
I catch them like snacks, come what may.

Realities whisper, but I'll hold them at bay,
When there's a donut or two on display.
With crumbs on my shirt and a yawn in the air,
I'll twirl through this life, without a care.

So join in the fun, share a bite or two,
Life will wait patiently; we've snacks to chew.
And as we nap, with smiles on our lips,
Let laughter and food be our sweetest trips.

Silken Camembert and Silent Thoughts

Silken cheese whispers, while I contemplate,
A life filled with snacks is a worthy fate.
Thoughts glide like crackers, crisp and divine,
With each little bite, I feel it align.

In corners of rooms, my dreams curl and bend,
As I dip into cheese, my faithful friend.
Naps hover nearby, soft as a sigh,
Together we thrive, like clouds in the sky.

I ponder the meaning of this merry feast,
Finding purpose in laughter, a joy-filled beast.
Not rushing through days, but savoring each crumb,
With a dash of humor, oh how I succumb!

So bring on the snacks, let the moments collide,
A palate of fun, in flavors we glide.
Amidst silent thoughts, I find my delight,
With laughter and cheese, the world feels just right.

Prelude to Rest

As the sun dips low, I prepare for my throne,
A cozy blanket, a snack, I'm not alone.
With chips in a bowl, and crumbs in my lap,
This is the good life, the ultimate nap.

I ponder if yogurt is really a treat,
Or just a smooth dance on a long, busy beat.
Naps beckon softly, their cozy allure,
Whispering secrets that make my heart pure.

Each tick of the clock, like a wave on the shore,
Takes me closer to snacks, and then a bit more.
The prelude to rest, like a sweet serenade,
With laughter and snacks, my worries will fade.

So gather 'round friends, let's revel and toast,
To quirky adventures, snacks we love most.
In this dance of delight, we're intertwined,
With bites and with naps, pure treasures we find.

Musing Under Shade and Snacks

In the shade with a bag of chips,
Time drifts by on savory trips.
A crunch, a grin, the world's all right,
My joy is found in bites tonight.

Sunshine warms the faded grass,
Tummy rumbles, snack time's a blast.
With soda pop and laughter near,
What could be better? Not a care here!

Lemonade spills, laughter flies,
A nap slips in through starry skies.
Beneath the sun, carefree we lay,
Tasting life in a funny way.

So here's to crumbs and whispers sweet,
Finding bliss in every treat.
Under trees where joy expands,
Life is grand with snack in hands.

The Quietude of Gelato Moments

Scoops of bliss on sunny days,
Melting treats in a sugary haze.
Chocolate drips and sprinkles fly,
Ice cream dreams make worries die.

With each spoon I take a sigh,
At this moment, I can't lie.
A quiet laugh, a happy dance,
In every taste, I find my chance.

The world around can just wait,
Cone in hand, oh, isn't it great?
Gelato smiles, twirls in the air,
Living fully without a care.

When the sun fades and skies turn gray,
I'll still savor ice cream's play.
For in these moments, I converse,
With sweet delight, and life's not adverse.

Siesta and Savor: A Duality

A cozy couch, the sun beaming bright,
I plop down for an afternoon light.
With pillows soft and worries at bay,
In dreamy land, snacks lead the way.

Peanut butter and jelly galore,
Nap time whispers, 'Can I have more?'
Chips underfoot, oh what a mess,
Caught between slumber and snackiness.

My eyes may close, my heart beats fast,
In this moment, I might just last.
With crumbs on my shirt, I drift anew,
Savoring rest, and snacks too!

When the clock strikes, I'll rise with cheer,
To chase the snacks that disappear.
A giggle shared, life's little games,
Dancing between naps and munching flames.

Snacking Through the Labyrinth

Wandering paths of savory dreams,
Through crunchy corners, laughter beams.
With popcorn in pocket, I make my way,
Exploring delights where flavors play.

Down chocolate lanes, my heart alive,
Guided by snacks, I take a dive.
In every twist, a new delight,
Golden French fries shine so bright.

Through marshmallow clouds, I float along,
With gummy bears, I can't go wrong.
Life's a maze, delicious and fun,
In every bite, I've already won.

As roars of laughter fill the air,
With silly dances, I haven't a care.
So onward I munch, through sweet and savory,
In this labyrinth, I'll always be free.

Musings on Morsels

When hunger strikes, I must confess,
Snacks become my happiness.
With chips and dips, I find my bliss,
Fried delights, I can't resist.

Naps call softly, sweet repose,
Dozing off, my eyelids close.
Between the bites, I dream so grand,
Of feasts and friends, a snacking band.

A cookie here, a cake slice there,
Life's little joys are everywhere.
In buttery bliss, I float and sway,
For snacks and snoozes save the day.

So let the world turn round with glee,
I'll gather snacks for you and me.
To munch, to nap, a perfect blend,
In buttercream, our hearts transcend.

Interludes of Introspection

Sipping soda, pondering fate,
Why do I procrastinate?
A nap here, a snack over there,
Philosophy's best done with flair.

Life's deep questions seem to fade,
Once I've had my cheese charade.
What's the meaning? Who really knows,
But nachos sure do cure my woes.

In cozy corners, I take my stand,
Munching popcorn, all unplanned.
Thoughts like candy, sweet yet rare,
Naps and snacks strip thoughts laid bare.

So here I sit, no need for grief,
With a sandwich or a beefy leaf.
From crumbs of wisdom, I will glean,
The joys of snacks are ever keen.

The Sweet Harmony of Hearth

In the kitchen, chaos reigns,
While cupcakes dance on candy trains.
Baking bread with sprinkles bright,
A warm embrace, pure heart's delight.

The kettle whistles, I'm off track,
Forget the stress, it's snack attack!
Happiness kneads with butter and flour,
Between every bite, I feel the power.

Cookies fresh out of the heat,
Laughter swirls on story's beat.
Naps in the sun, with warmth so sweet,
With treats aplenty, life feels complete.

So raise a toast to joy and cheer,
With every nibble, hold friends near.
Let's dine in laughter, may it be clear,
That snacks and hugs bring us here.

Chasing Dreams Between Crumbs

In the chase for dreams, there's much ado,
But first, a bite of something new.
Muffins piled on plates so high,
Fueling my whims like clouds in the sky.

Naps are golden, a cozy retreat,
Where visions dance and flavors meet.
I slumber soft with cookie dreams,
Between each bite, the laughter beams.

Pies that whisper, "Have one more,"
Draw me closer to that blissful shore.
Each crumb like hope, a journey begun,
I'm after dreams and sticky buns.

So let me snack, let me doze,
In a cupcake haze, my spirit grows.
For in the chase where crumbs may fall,
I'll savor each one, answering the call.

Savoring the In-Between

In the space where snacks collide,
I find my joy, I can't hide.
Chips may crumble, dips may spill,
Yet it's a feast of pure goodwill.

With popcorn skies and candy dreams,
Life's a banquet, or so it seems.
From savory bites to sweet delight,
I munch away, my soul takes flight.

Laughter echoes with each crunch,
Every nibble feels like a punch.
In this dance of flavors, I sway,
Celebrating each quirky, tasty day.

In between, where moments rest,
I savor each bite, and feel so blessed.
For in this chaos, I take my stand,
With snacks in hand, life's simply grand.

The Joy of a Well-Placed Nap

As I nestle in a comfy chair,
The world outside just fades to air.
With a yawn so deep, I close an eye,
In dreamland's grip, I learn to fly.

Time stops tickin', worries cease,
In this cocoon, I find my peace.
Floating on clouds, no care in sight,
Every snooze feels just so right.

A well-placed nap, my secret prize,
Beneath the sunlit afternoon skies.
With pillow soft and dreams so sweet,
I recharge my soul, then rise to eat.

Awake I spring, with snacks in tow,
Refreshed and ready for a show.
In the pause of slumber's gentle clasp,
I feast on joy, and then I gasp.

Cradled by Comfort Foods

With a bowl of goodness in my lap,
I find my solace, take a nap.
Mac and cheese, a warm embrace,
In every bite, I find my place.

Chewy cookies, oh what a thrill,
Each crumb delivers such a chill.
Burgers piled with love so grand,
In comfort foods, I take my stand.

Ice cream rivers, sweet delight,
I float along, through day and night.
Savoring flavors, a hearty spoon,
In this feast, I dance like a loon.

Cradled by meals, my heart sings loud,
Amidst the chaos, I feel so proud.
For in each taste, the world unwinds,
In comfort foods, pure joy I find.

Reveries on a Blanket

A blanket spread on grassy green,
Where dreams are stitched, and snacks are seen.
With sandwiches nestled snug and tight,
We munch and laugh, what pure delight!

In sun-drenched spots, with lemonade,
The worries float, and silence fades.
Chasing crumbs, like little sprites,
We relish in these sunny sights.

With giggles bursting in the air,
A picnic party, nothing can compare.
As we nibble bites and stretch out wide,
In simple joys, we take our stride.

Underneath the bright blue skies,
We savor moments, let worries die.
For on this blanket, bonds are made,
In laughter's embrace, we find our trade.

Reveries in a Bubble of Rest

In a hammock, dreams collide,
With snacks beside—a joyful ride.
Twirling thoughts like cotton candy,
Napping feels just like a dandy.

Floating high on sugary clouds,
Where quiet giggles break the crowds.
With sleepy sighs, the time just bends,
A laugh, a snack, where fun transcends.

Pillowed up, with dips and chips,
My mind drifts off on tasty trips.
Tickled toes and sunny rays,
Just snore away the busy days.

In the end, it's all a blur,
A dance of crumbs and soft whirrs.
With every bite and sleepy glance,
A playful life is but a chance.

Crumbs on the Cumulus

On fluffy clouds, I take my seat,
With cookie crumbs—oh, such a treat!
As marshmallows drift by for a ride,
I munch and snooze with joy and pride.

Biscuit dreams on cotton skies,
I dive into a snack surprise.
A nap to blend with sugary bliss,
Each bite feels like a gentle kiss.

Snoozing lightly in a breeze,
Grazing snacks with perfect ease.
Laughter lingers through the air,
In this sweet slumber, without a care.

With crumbs to catch and dreams to weave,
This cloud-based joy, I dare believe.
It's humor wrapped in fluffy layers,
My snack-filled naps—oh, what players!

The Serenity of a Sleepy Afternoon

In afternoon's gentle embrace,
I seek the cozy, quiet space.
Where chips and dips find their home,
And whisk me off to dreamland's dome.

A yawning stretch, a sleepy sigh,
While munching popcorn, oh me, oh my!
The world fades soft like buttercream,
As I snuggle into a snack-filled dream.

With chocolate fingers, I dive deep,
Into a ticket for a dreamy sleep.
Naps are sneaky, snacks on cue,
The perfect blend of rest anew.

As cookies crinkle in my dreams,
I float along in sunlit beams.
A curious mix of rest and cheer,
Where every snack feels like a dear.

Tastefully Tranquil

In a world of chips and cheese galore,
I find my peace and so much more.
With every nibble comes a grin,
In this serene dance, I just begin.

Napkin shields and crumbs afloat,
A buffet while I love to dote.
Soft pillows cradle lazy days,
With laughter echoing in playful ways.

Twinkling eyes, the clock slows down,
In laughter's embrace, forget the frown.
A sandwich hug, a muffin's kiss,
Who knew tranquility could taste like this?

So here I sit, a joyous sight,
With snacks that sparkle in the light.
Life, it seems, is best when shared,
With fluffy naps and snacks prepared.

Twilight Tastes

In twilight's glow, we munch away,
With cookies, cakes, and chips at play.
Laughter rings, the world's our feast,
Where worries vanish, love's released.

We chat of dreams and silly things,
Like flying cats and diamond rings.
With every bite, a giggle flows,
In twilight's realm, pure joy bestows.

Each snack's a treasure, crisp and sweet,
A sweet escape from daily heat.
While napping's art is perfection's mark,
We blend delight with a sprinkle of spark.

Confections and Contemplations

Chocolate truffles make us think,
About that time we spilled our drink.
With jellybeans and goofy glares,
Life's questions melt, the taste still dares.

A cupcake here, a frown erased,
With icing dreams, our fears are faced.
We ponder sweets, not deep schticks,
And find the joy in sugar tricks.

As thoughts get wrapped in caramel bliss,
We munch and muse, oh what a twist!
With laughter bright, we share our bites,
In scrumptious moments, we find delights.

The Nap Between the Bites

Between the munch and cozy snooze,
We find the best of chews and blues.
A little daze, a quick dessert,
With giggles shared, there's never hurt.

A cookie crunch, then off we go,
To find a nap, to dream and flow.
With snacks at hand and pillows near,
A rhythm blooms, there's nothing to fear.

The balance swings from bite to rest,
In every taste, we seek the best.
So between the laughs, we seek that dream,
In a foodie haze, life's a happy theme.

Filled with Fragments

With pretzel sticks and tales so bright,
We munch on bits of pure delight.
Fragments of joy in every crunch,
We find the magic in each lunch.

As crumbs fall down and laughter swells,
The stories spark like jumbled bells.
A snack's embrace, a cozy chat,
In fragments found, we're simply that.

With sweet surprises and chips galore,
We share our hearts and then explore.
Caught in munching, we fade to dreams,
And build a life with silly themes.

The Restful Intermission

In the middle of a busy day,
A comfy couch calls out, hooray!
With chips in hand and soda too,
I take a break, how 'bout you?

The clock ticks on, but who really cares?
As snacks and naps are mine to share.
With pillows piled, I drift and dream,
Life's a pause, or so it seems.

The afternoon sun beams through the blinds,
The perfect moment for relaxed minds.
I munch away, and woozy I fall,
To the dance of snack crumbs in the hall.

So let's embrace this restful interlude,
With playful snacks and none of the brood.
For every nap, a treat must wait,
In this silly dance, I celebrate!

Thoughts as Flavors

What's on my mind? A swirling mix,
Of chocolate, popcorn, and salty tricks.
Each thought pops like a kernel in heat,
   Mmmm, it's savory, can't be beat!

   Ideas drift in a buttery haze,
   Like nachos cheese on lazy days.
Some spicy, some sweet, all on a plate,
   What's next to dip? It's up to fate!

   Is it nap time, or time to eat?
These flavors blend in a tasty feat.
With sleepy dreams and crunchy bites,
   A world of joy consists of delights.

Let's mix and match this buffet of thought,
   In the flavor game, I am never caught.
   Eating, resting, thoughts sailing by,
   In this deliciousness, I find my high.

Patterns of Leisure

On the fabric of my daily grind,
I stitch together naps, it's kind.
With patterns woven of joy and rest,
Snacking on chips, it's truly the best.

A quilt of comfort, bright with glee,
Where popcorn and pillows go wild, you see.
Each little nap brings a burst of cheer,
As I dream of tacos dancing near.

Sundays filled with a lazy grace,
Pajamas worn like a snug embrace.
Snacks by my side, laughter in air,
Tickle my toes, forget the care.

Join the fun in this tapestry,
Where the only rule is to be carefree.
For in these patterns, a blissful wrap,
Lie the stitches of joy — a frothy nap!

An Afternoon of Delicious Distractions

In the afternoon glow, the snacks unfold,
Every corner reveals treasures untold.
With gummy bears lining up in a queue,
It's a feast fit for me and you!

A distraction here, a cookie there,
Naps sneak in, like they own the chair.
Chocolate bars whisper sweet lullabies,
While sleepy heads begin to rise.

The clock winks at us, "Why not slow down?"
As donut sprinkles dance around town.
Each bite beckons a moment to pause,
In this leisurely spot, there's no cause.

As life steams by like a fresh pot brewed,
I'll savor the snacks that make me feel good.
In the laughter and crumbs from delightful chats,
It's here in distraction, my heart tips its hats!

Serenade of the Scone

In the morning light I rise,
Scone in hand, and dream of skies.
Butter melts like good advice,
Crumbs fall softly, oh so nice.

Tea brews warm on the stove's tune,
A cozy chair, a lazy afternoon.
With sweet raspberry hope in my bite,
All my worries take flight!

The world can wait, I'll just unwind,
Between each nibble, peace I find.
Filling my heart with tasty things,
Listening closely to joy it brings.

A serenade of biscuits and jam,
I live like a warm, contented clam.
If life's a dish, I'd take my pick:
One more scone, then cozy nap quick!

Nibbles and Daydreams

With popcorn scattered on my lap,
I sail away into a nap.
Each crunch a ticket to my dreams,
Where nothing is quite as it seems.

Chasing snacks on a sugar high,
Chocolate whispers from nearby.
I ponder life with fluffy clouds,
Amidst the snacks, my heart allows.

Between each nibble, thoughts take flight,
Daydreaming in pure delight.
Potato chips can cure the blues,
Crunching loud, I'll take the snooze.

Sweet and savory, my heart sings,
In this realm of trivial things.
Life's great joy is clear, it seems,
In the middle of munchies and dreams.

The Cozy Interlude

Wrapped in blankets, soft and tight,
With muffins basking in the light.
Each crumb whispers, 'Take your time',
Savor moments, sweet as rhyme.

The kettle hums a gentle tune,
A dance of flavors, morning's boon.
With every sip, my cares dissolve,
In this warm world, I feel resolve.

A quick escape from daily grind,
In pastries' warmth, joy I find.
Napkin crumpled, but heart so full,
In cozy corners, dreams do pull.

So let the worries trip and fall,
As I enjoy this snack-filled ball.
In these quiet moments spent,
I find my joys, my heart's content.

Reflections Over a Coffee Break

Between the sips and gentle swirls,
Life's chaos pauses, in curls and twirls.
With donuts dancing on the tray,
I ponder all the whims today.

Coffee's warmth, a snug embrace,
Time slows down; I find my place.
A laugh with cream, a joke with cake,
In every sip, some bliss I make.

Each muffin crumb a part of me,
A soft reminder to just be free.
In the middle of this tasty quest,
I find my joy, I find my rest.

So here's to breaks and laughter shared,
In every nibble, love declared.
With you beside, it's all a treat,
Reflections sweet, that can't compete.

The Breath Between the Chews

In a world of bites and giggles,
We munch and chuckle, savoring the wiggles.
Each crunch a blessing, each sip divine,
A snack in hand, oh how we dine!

The crumbs may fall, we won't despair,
For laughter's sweetness fills the air.
We pause to breathe, we take a break,
In the joy of food, our hearts awake!

Beneath the stars, with treats we share,
Our tummies full, without a care.
Each moment cherished, we take our time,
Life's a feast, and oh, how we rhyme!

So raise your snacks, let's spread the cheer,
In this playful dance, we have nothing to fear.
With every nibble, let giggles rise,
For in each bite, our laughter flies!

A Tapestry of Comfort and Calm

In cozy corners, we nest and find,
A blanket, a snack, a peaceful mind.
With crumbs on our shirts, and a grin so wide,
We sit back, relax, let comfort be our guide.

With cups of cocoa, the world's a blur,
In sweet indulgence, we never incur.
The whispers of pillows, a soft embrace,
In laughter and munchies, we find our place.

Our worries drift with each sugary bite,
As naptime beckons, we welcome the night.
The joy of stillness, a belly full,
In our tapestry of calm, life's never dull.

So frolic through meadows of cotton and cream,
With snacks and sweet dreams, we'll make our team.
As laughter lingers, hugs intertwine,
A world of comfort, together we shine!

Serendipity on a Soft Pillow

Embrace the day with a lazy smile,
A cookie here, a nap worthwhile.
With crumbs on our cheeks and dreams so sweet,
In slumber's arms, we find our treat.

Bubbles of laughter dance in dreams,
We wander through fields of sugary creams.
With every slumber, joy takes flight,
In the land of fluff, everything feels right.

Pillow forts rise, a castle so fine,
With snacks on the throne, our joys entwine.
With giggles we sip from our comfort zone,
In this whimsical world, we have grown.

As the sun dips low, we close our eyes,
In a cozy cocoon, the laughter lies.
So rest easy, dear friend, with snacks in tow,
In serendipity's bliss, let the good times flow!

The Poetry of Half-Closed Eyes

With half-closed eyes and a snack in hand,
We drift through dreams in a wonderland.
The crunchy echoes are our serenade,
As we lounge and ponder, in delight we wade.

In the stillness, a giggle slips free,
A feast of the mind, just you and me.
With every nibble, we float on clouds,
In comfy corners, we silence the crowds.

The sun softly dances, the world fades away,
As snacks become verses in sweet ballet.
In the poetry written with crumbs and sighs,
We find all the truths beneath sunny skies.

So let's raise our voices, let laughter ring,
In half-closed eyes, joys brightly cling.
With snacks and dreams, we'll forge our way,
In this hilarious tale, we'll gladly stay!

Biscuit Dreams and Blanket Haze

In the morning I rise, but not very fast,
Pancakes are calling, I dream of the past.
Fluffy clouds in my coffee, a sip and a sigh,
Do I really need plans? I'll just eat and lie.

Squishy pillows surround me, oh what a sight,
A symphony of crumbs gives my heart such delight.
With biscuits beside me, I hold my ground,
In a kingdom of snacks, I'm the king, I'm renowned.

The TV hums softly, a warm, cozy tune,
Laughter and snacks, a magical room.
What's on today's menu? I ponder and dream,
A couch full of wonders, just me and my cream.

As the sunset approaches, I stretch and I yawn,
In this biscuit-filled haze, I'll rest till the dawn.
The world can wait softly, with moments so grand,
My throne is my blanket, my kingdom so planned.

Culinary Daydreams

I wander through kitchens, a sweet savory land,
Whisking my worries with a butter-filled hand.
Cupcakes and cookies dance under the light,
In the fantasy kitchen, everything's bright.

With spoons full of sugar and pots full of glee,
I scoop up the laughter; it's better with tea.
A chef's hat of fluffiness, wear it with pride,
In this oven of joy, I'm the chef and the guide.

I bake in my slippers; it's a cozy affair,
Sticky fingers and flour, no worries to bear.
Brownies in the oven, their scent fills the room,
I smile at the chaos, it starts to bloom.

When the last crumb is gone and my belly is round,
I plop on the sofa; oh, bliss can be found!
In culinary daydreams, I find my delight,
With snacks as my allies, I'll linger all night.

The Sweetness of Staying Still

A warm blanket wraps me, it feels like a hug,
Cuddled up tight, like a well-fed bug.
The sun shines through softly, a lazy low beam,
In this sweetness of stillness, I float like a dream.

Cookies are calling from a platter nearby,
Oh, what am I doing? Just watching time fly.
Nap time is beckoning, oh what a sweet theft,
As I drift off with visions of chocolate, I'm swept.

The clock barely ticks, it slows down for me,
In this moment of pure joy, I choose to just be.
The sweetness of staying still is quite the delight,
With snacks in my grasp, I'll savor the night.

As the stars start to twinkle and the world grows dim,
I snuggle in deeper, feeling blissfully slim.
With every bite savored, my heart starts to swell,
In the sweetness of stillness, all is just swell.

Embracing the Sluggish Hours

Slowly the day flows like molasses, you see,
With naps tucked in pockets, they're calling for me.
A burrito of blankets, I wrap myself tight,
Embracing the sluggish hours, oh what a sight.

The couch has a pull like a warm summer breeze,
With snacks in my lap, I find it a breeze.
Chips and some salsa, all piled up high,
I munch and I crunch while I let out a sigh.

The minutes grow lazy, each moment's a treat,
As I nestle in comfort, I'm feeling complete.
Adventures can wait while I enjoy this phase,
In embrace of the sluggish, life simply displays.

So here's to the hours that meander so slow,
With laughter and crumbs, let the good times flow.
In this whimsical dance, the world's in my palm,
With snacks and sweet slumbers, I'm filled up with calm.

Balancing Crumbs and Comfort

In the kitchen, snacks abound,
Pillow forts where dreams are found.
A chip in hand, a nap in store,
Snoozing hard, till crumbs hit the floor.

Chasing snacks while time flies by,
With every bite, a satisfied sigh.
Dreams of cookies, chips galore,
Who knew comfort came from the core?

Balancing joy, with a belly full,
Stumbling naps, feeling quite dull.
Laughing loud, with gleeful cheer,
Counting calories without a fear.

For every snack, there's a peaceful doze,
Life's just better when you take it slow.
A balance struck, with mismatched socks,
Delight in crumbs and sleepy clocks.

A Symphony of Stillness

Quiet tunes of a snack time bliss,
Napping softly, no need to miss.
Crunching sounds like a sweet serenade,
As slumbers weave a cozy parade.

Potato chips in a quiet crunch,
Silent dreams in a midday lunch.
Harmony found in both crunch and yawn,
With each new flavor, a sleepy dawn.

A lullaby of munching delight,
Cuddled up, we take flight.
Melodies dance on comfy cushions,
In a world where snacks are the best missions.

Oh, the joy in each drowsy bite,
A funny twist to the day and night.
Let us snack and drift away,
In sweet stillness, we'll always stay.

The Dance of Rest and Relish

Restful rhythms in the afternoon,
Chips and dips make the best tune.
Swaying gently to the snacktime beat,
Napping softly with a crumbly treat.

A waltz of tastes, a tango of zest,
In comfy chairs, we find our rest.
Nibbles echo, as eyelids close,
In this sweet waltz, anything goes.

Step right up to a sleepy rhyme,
Where savory shades dance with sublime.
Twirling snacks on a lazy day,
Who knew rest could be such a play?

So let's embrace each sprinkle and snack,
With heart-filled laughter, there's no lack.
In the dance of flavors, dreams take flight,
Crumbs and comforts, a delight!

Echoes of Midday Respite

In the hush of afternoon light,
Chasing snacks feels just right.
Glimmers of laughter fill the air,
As naps whisper without a care.

Cookies crumbled, laughter spreads,
Dreamy moments pass like threads.
Naps wrapped tight in softest sheets,
Crumbs hidden in cozy retreats.

A slice of cake, a dash of fun,
Snoozing gently till day is done.
Echoes of munching in the sun,
Both snacks and sleep make hearts run.

So gather 'round for a biscuit feast,
Blend joy with slumber, at the very least.
Life's sweet echoes call us near,
In crumbs and comfort, we find cheer.

Savoring the Spaces In-Between

In the interlude of a nap,
Dreams mingle with crumbs and gap.
Snooze, then snack, it's quite a dance,
Juggling treats while in a trance.

Each chip and dip, a fleeting cheer,
A laugh, a crunch, it's crystal clear.
We find our bliss in cozy sighs,
With couch and snacks, we touch the skies.

A coffee sip, a sleepy grin,
Moments made before we begin.
Happiness rests on a plate,
Between the bites, we contemplate.

So take your time, embrace the pause,
With every snack, the world just draws.
The heart beats softly, all is right,
In munch and doze, we find our light.

The Palette of Pause

A sprinkle of chips, a dash of cheese,
Creating a feast that aims to please.
In colors bold, our plates align,
Between the bites, everything's fine.

Pudding swirls in a cozy bowl,
Pausing life's spin to fill the soul.
With laughter shared at every snack,
Time halts a bit, there's no lack.

While napping softly, dreams collide,
A hidden snack is as good as a ride.
Cracker crumbles on the thumb,
As we savor each tiny crumb.

So dip, delve in, and take a break,
A joyful heart is all it takes.
In simple meals and witty chats,
We find our joy, and that is that.

Nostalgia on a Biscuit

A cookie warm brings back the days,
Of childhood games and carefree ways.
With every bite, a memory wakes,
In buttery bliss, our heart aches.

Frosting smiles on a sugary treat,
Reflecting the past in every sweet.
Laughter and crumbs fall on the floor,
We can't help but crave just one more.

Sipping tea with a biscuit's hug,
Reminding us all of a warm drug.
Time melts slow with flavors unique,
In every nibble, we softly peak.

So raise a toast to those old times,
With chocolate chips and silly rhymes.
In every morsel, a tale we find,
A journey back to a simpler mind.

Unwinding with a Dainty Bite

A tiny tart on a fancy plate,
In small delights, we celebrate.
With laughter mixed in every cream,
We weave our dreams, a sweet esteem.

A cupcake here, a scone right there,
Delightful tastes float through the air.
With giggles shared at every nib,
Our worries fade, no need to fib.

A chocolate square sparkles bright,
As couch potatoes ease the night.
With sprinkles galore and icing swirls,
The cheeky joy in this world unfurls.

So take a bite and share a laugh,
Let's savor this whimsical photograph.
In dainty bites, we find our cheer,
With snacks and naps, it's all so dear.

Harmonies of Hibernation

In the cozy nest we find our peace,
Dreams of cheese and crunchy peas.
As snores blend softly with the snack's crunch,
We contemplate the world over lunch.

Pajamas on and slippers too,
The only agenda? More food to chew.
Chasing crumbs with sleepy eyes,
Harmonies of joy in our sighs.

So let the couch be our throne,
Where in comfy bliss we've brightly grown.
With pillows piled like mountains too,
The art of relaxation is our cue.

The clock ticks slow as time unwinds,
In pursuit of nibbles, our joy we find.
Hibernation's hymn—loud and clear,
Nibble, snooze, repeat—bring on the cheer!

Minutes Between Nibbles

The clock strikes snack time, oh what a sight,
A glorious feast in the soft, dim light.
With fingers sticky and laughter bright,
We munch away until the next day's bite.

A moment to ponder, just after a meal,
How many snacks give that perfect feel?
From chips to dips, each salty thrill,
In the hunt for crunch, we find our will.

Between sips of soda and bites of pie,
We pause and giggle, oh me, oh my!
For moments like these, we live and laugh,
Perfecting each munch like a tasty craft.

So here's to the seconds when we indulge,
In flavors and textures, let the joy bulge.
With crumbs on our shirts, and glee in our hearts,
Minutes between nibbles—where the fun starts!

The Pondering Pita

Oh pita bread, you carry dreams,
A vessel for all culinary themes.
Stuffed with goodies, we ponder and fill,
Life's greatest questions, between each thrill.

Is it better to snack or take a nap?
Debating this over a cheesy wrap.
As we stack toppings, our spirits soar,
Leaving our worries at the kitchen door.

In laughter we crumble, the spices blend,
Each bite a journey, each flavor a friend.
With garlic and veggies, it's hard to resist,
Philosophy fades like a well-earned mist.

So we chew on questions of how to please,
While relishing wraps from the world with ease.
For in these moments, oh what a treat,
The pondering pita makes life complete!

Reverie Wrapped in a Blanket

Nestled snug like a burrito tight,
A blanket cocoon for the cozy night.
With snacks beside me and dreams on my mind,
Here's to the moments of bliss I find.

Each chip I munch whispers a tale,
In the whispering folds where comfort prevails.
Tangled in folds and savory bites,
Reveries dance in the soft golden lights.

Adventures abound in a world so vast,
But for now, let's enjoy this blanket cast.
With popcorn clouds and chips like stars,
We sail on dreams from our couch to Mars.

So wrap me in comfort, let worries cease,
Between munches and snuggles, we find our peace.
With every nap and snack, we create a trance,
These moments of joy make the heart dance!

The Delicate Dance of Indulgence

With chips in hand, I sway and groove,
As cookies call, I make my move.
The crunch, the munch, a tasty delight,
In this grand ballet of snack-filled night.

Balancing dreams on a mountain of cheese,
With every bite, my worries freeze.
Oh, to twirl in chocolate's embrace,
Finding joy in this delectable space.

The salsa dips, the nachos cheer,
A rhapsody of flavors, oh so near.
But can I juggle bites and brief naps?
In this comedic circus, no time for traps!

When snoring starts, the popcorn flies,
I laugh aloud under snack-filled skies.
For in this dance, it's clear to see,
The thrill of indulgence sets my spirit free.

Between Bites and Breaths

In the kitchen, I make my stand,
A gathering of snacks, oh so grand.
Between each crunch and joyful sigh,
I ponder if it's time to fly.

A potato chip here, a gumdrop there,
In this sweet chaos, I declare!
I nibble, I munch, then pause for air,
Regaining strength for moments rare.

Oh, the art of biting, the beauty of chips,
Fueling my thoughts, igniting my quips.
With every taste, a laugh to find,
In this snack-filled world, so hilariously kind!

So, here's the secret, the riddle I keep,
Between bites and breaths, I happily leap.
For life's a buffet, a whimsical game,
And each snack is a badge, a claim to fame.

Epiphanies on the Couch

On the couch, I settle deep,
With popcorn close, I'll surely leap.
In my thoughts, a grand parade,
As crumbs and dreams begin to trade.

The remote in hand, the snacks in sight,
A flicker of wisdom, oh what a night!
As I ponder flavor, my mind takes flight,
In the kingdom of comfort, all feels right.

Here, inspiration flows like soda pop,
In between chips, I learn, I stop.
A glorious mess, a delightful view,
As I contemplate all that I chew.

With each tasty bite, new thoughts arise,
Who knew the couch held such sweet surprise?
So I'll snack and snooze, my trusty throne,
In this whimsical world, I've found my own.

A Midnight Cookie Manifesto

At midnight's hour, the cookies sing,
A chorus sweet, oh the joy they bring.
With stealth and grace, I make my claim,
In the pantry's depths, they know my name.

Choco chips and oatmeal flair,
Each batch crafted with loving care.
I nibble softly, not to wake,
It's a cookie heist, for goodness' sake!

With every bite, a revolution starts,
A manifesto written in cookie hearts.
I shall not hide, nor shall I wait,
For midnight munchies, I celebrate.

So raise a glass of milk so frothy,
For cookie truth, so sweet and lofty.
In this late-night romp, joyfully absurd,
I stand united with snacks, undeterred.

www.ingramcontent.com/pod-product-compliance
Lightning Source LLC
Chambersburg PA
CBHW051659160426
43209CB00004B/957